A Beginner's Guide to

WILDFLOWERS
OF THE C&O TOWPATH

—— *A Beginner's Guide to* ——
WILDFLOWERS
OF THE C&O TOWPATH

Text and Photographs by
EDWIN M. MARTIN

Smithsonian Institution Press
Washington, D.C.

Audubon Naturalist Society
of the Central Atlantic States
1984

Editor: Deborah E. Corsi
Designer: Alan Carter

Library of Congress Cataloging in Publication Data

Martin, Edwin M. (Edwin McCammon)
  A beginner's guide to wildflowers of the C&O towpath.

  Bibliography: p.
  Includes index.
  1. Wildflowers—Chesapeake and Ohio Canal (Md. and
Washington, D.C.)—Identification.   I. Title.
QK165.M37 1984   582.13'09752'84   83-20314
ISBN 0-87474-657-4 (pbk.)

The paper in this book meets the guidelines for permanence and
durability of the Committee on Production Guidelines for Book
Longevity of the Council on Library Resources.

Black-and-white line drawings are by Alice Tangerini and were
adapted from illustrations in the following publications with the
permission of the publishers:
Roadside Flowers of Texas, Mary M. Willis and Howard S. Irvin, ©
1961 by University of Texas Press.
*Field Guide to Wildflowers of Northeastern and North-Central North
America*, © 1968 by Roger Tory Peterson and Margaret McKenny;
Houghton Mifflin Company, publisher.
Field Guide to Pacific States Wildflowers, © 1976 by Theodore F.
Niehaus and Charles L. Ripper; Houghton Mifflin Company,
publisher.
Newcomb's Wildflower Guide, Lawrence Newcomb, © 1977 by
Little, Brown and Company.

CONTENTS

ACKNOWLEDGMENTS

Many people have made important contributions to this guide. The idea for it came from Adam Foster in the winter of 1981 at a Maryland Nature Conservancy fund-raising event. Adam, who had been with me in the late '50s at the U.S. Embassy in London, learned that I enjoyed wildflower photography as a hobby, and called my attention to the fact that there was no wildflower guide for users of the C&O Towpath. He spoke as a D.C. representative on both the Potomac River Commission and the Advisory Council to the Superintendent of the C&O Canal Historical Park.

At his suggestion, I first checked out the proposal with Franziska Hecht, a Park Service official who served as the executive secretary of the Friends of Parks and Monuments of Metropolitan Washington. She urged me to tackle it.

Then a former colleague in the Foreign Service started, and has continued to give me encouragement and good advice. I refer to E.F. Rivinus, former director of Smithsonian Institution Press, and once a board chairman of the Audubon Naturalist Society.

A key source of help throughout has been Stanwyn Shetler, curator of botany at the Smithsonian Institution, also a former chairman of the Audubon Naturalist Society board, and currently a colleague of mine on it. He is also an inspiring leader of botanical forays.

Others to whom I am indebted include C&O Historical Park Superintendent Richard N. Stanton and several of his rangers, especially Chris Baumann; Carrie Johnson, chairman of the Advisory Council to the Superintendent of the C&O Canal Historical Park; Claudine Wirths, a flower lover and photographer especially devoted to the creation and preservation of Seneca State Park; Samuel Rainey, a Navy physicist who has become a major authority on the flowers of the Potomac basin; Daniel Boone, a top expert on all the flora of Maryland who serves on the staff of the Maryland Natural Heritage Program of the state government; and Gay MacKintosh, executive director of the Audubon Naturalist Society. Getting it all down on paper was made much easier by Deirdre Ward, a true expert at the word processor. I, of course, am responsible for the final text.

Last but by no means least, I have had constant support and help from my wife, Peggy, especially in covering the previously unknown areas north of Seneca. It involved a good deal of driving and the cooperation of her sharp eyes in order to quickly take the needed census of blooming plants so that other locations could be covered before we returned to Washington.

The publication of this book was made possible by the Smithsonian Institution, and the Audubon Naturalist Society of the Central Atlantic States. Its quality has been much improved by the editorial and design skills of the staff of the Smithsonian Institution Press.

INTRODUCTION

This beginner's guide contains descriptions and color photos of 120 species of flowering plants, plus descriptions of 38 similar species, that I saw in bloom on the C&O Towpath at eight selected points between Georgetown and Cumberland: Locks 5–7, Anglers Inn–Great Falls, Seneca, Edwards Ferry, Point of Rocks, Sharpsburg, Paw Paw, and Spring Gap–North Branch. They were each covered at approximately one month intervals from April to October 1982. As background for this guide, I frequently walked on the towpath from Seneca south in search of new species over the past eight years.

From my experience I can suggest that the number of species in bloom at any one time is plentiful throughout April and May, relatively poor in June, picks up in July, and hits its peak in August and September. This is especially true in the area from Seneca south where a two-hour walk can result in sightings of as many as sixty different species in bloom. I found the greatest variety of species throughout the year along the Anglers Inn–Great Falls stretch, and the path over the Paw Paw tunnel is bordered by many species not found elsewhere on the towpath.

To keep the guide to a convenient size and cost, hard choices had to be made from more than 200 species seen. In addition to frequency of sighting, preference was given to those species whose flowers are easily seen and to those found below Seneca where traffic on the towpath tends to be heaviest. I have also included a few species that are not common but have flowers that are worth seeing.

Differences among the species found at the eight points covered were fewer than I had expected, those blooming north of Seneca differing little from those to the south. There are, however, a greater number of species south of Seneca where it is sunnier. Here the canal bed is filled with water; in the north it is usually filled with trees.

Every author hopes that the demand for his book will require a second edition. Consequently, I welcome suggestions for improvement so that such a new edition might be a better guide.

To users of this book it is probably unnecessary to emphasize that these flowers will continue to provide enjoyment to all towpath users only if they are not disturbed.

How to use this guide

The easiest way to identify the flower you have seen is to compare it with the color photograph in the back of this book. The photographs are in order by the color of a plant's flower, and are keyed by number to the species descriptions. In each case only the first flower listed is represented by a photograph.

Included in each description are the species' popular and botanical names. The species are listed first by color, and then as follows:

Flowers Irregular
Flowers Regular
  Parts Easy to Count
  Parts Hard to Count

(Note: "parts" refers to petals, sepals, or rays)

Within the *irregular* and *regular* headings, the species are described in the following order: first by leaf placement beginning with alternate, followed by opposite, whorled, and basal. Within each leaf placement category, the descriptions are further in order by the number of parts of the flower, where that can readily be determined, starting with the fewest.

At the end of each description, are the first months of blooming in the Washington, D.C., area followed by the common family name of each species.

Where appropriate, the descriptions contain notes on present or former uses and on the origin of names.

The term "flower" is used in this guide the way most of us use it in daily conversation, that is, to refer to an iris, or sweet pea, or daisy. This usage is not technically accurate as a daisy "flower" is in fact a cluster of small flowers. This is true of all members of the daisy family. Nearly all of them have rays that look like a many-petaled flower, but it is an illusion.

stamen

- anther
- filament

- axil
- stalk
- stem

- bract

irregular flowers

lobed

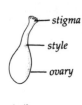

- stigma
- style
- ovary

pistil

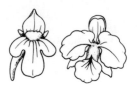

palmate

- sepal

- spur

- stipule

toothed

whorled

GLOSSARY

Anther	The sac-like structure at the top of a thread-like filament that contains the pollen. Together the anther and filament are called the stamen, the male organ of a flower.
Axil	The point (top side) where a leaf or its stalk joins the main stem.
Bract	Small leaflike structures between a flower and the true leaves. Usually green. Found most frequently with flowers of the daisy family.
Entire	A leaf with smooth edges.
Irregular	A flower with petals that form an unsymmetrical structure around a central point.
Lobed	A leaf with deep, angular or curved indentations.
Palmate	A leaf divided into leaflets arranged around a stalk like fingers around a palm. Usually there are five but there may be from three to nine leaflets.
Part	Refers usually to petals but in some cases to colored sepals that are almost indistinguishable from petals. In the case of the daisy family "part" refers to the single conspicuous petal-like ray of all or some of the many flowers that make up its inflorescence.
Pistil	The female organ of a flower, consisting of an ovary, one or more styles, and a stigma.
Regular	A flower with petals that form a symmetrical structure around a central point.
Sepal	A petal-shaped, typically green structure just outside the petals. It sometimes occurs in other colors and replaces all or some of the petals.
Spur	A backward or downward extension of a petal or sepal.
Stalk	The structure that connects a leaf or a flower to the stem of a plant.
Stamen	The male organ of a flower composed of a thread-like filament and an anther.
Stem	The main axis of a plant from which leaves and flowers develop.

Stigma	The tip of the pistil, it receives the pollen that fertilizes the ovules in the ovary.
Stipule	Small, paired leaflike structures found in some species at the base of a leafstalk.
Style	The slender stalk of the pistil.
Toothed	A leaf with teethlike projections along its edges.
Whorled	Three or more leaves attached to a stem at the same point.

LEAF IDENTIFICATION GUIDE

Leaves grow in a variety of shapes that are useful aids to identification. The most common (illustrated below) are linear, lanceolate, oval, egg-shaped, and heart-shaped.

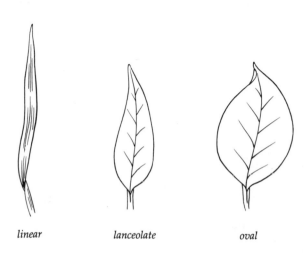

linear   *lanceolate*   *oval*

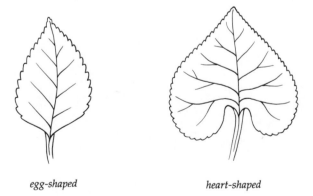

egg-shaped   *heart-shaped*

THE C&O TOWPATH

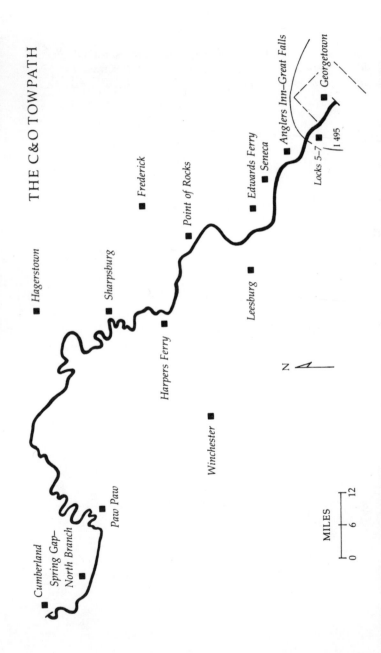

Cumberland

Spring Gap–
North Branch

Paw Paw

Hagerstown

Sharpsburg

Harpers Ferry

Winchester

Frederick

Point of Rocks

Leesburg

Edwards Ferry

Seneca

Anglers Inn–Great Falls

Locks 5–7

I 495

Georgetown

N

MILES

0   6   12

WHITE

FLOWERS IRREGULAR

1. **White Sweet Clover** *(Melilotus alba)* is 3'–8' tall and often grows in large clumps. Its alternate leaves have three finely toothed leaflets. The pealike flowers grow on many, slender, tapering, 2"–4" spikes, which rise from the leaf axils and terminate the stem. From Europe. Brought to America by beekeepers as its nectar makes fine honey. *Meli* means honey in Greek. (June–Sept., Pea)

2. **Pale Violet, Cream Violet** *(Viola striata)* has a flower growing on a long stalk from a leaf axil. There are purplish veins at the base of each petal. The alternate leaves are heart-shaped, also on long stalks. At the leaf axils there are relatively large and deeply toothed stipules. (Apr.–May, Violet)

3. **Japanese Honeysuckle** *(Lonicera japonica)* is a vine that climbs everywhere—over bushes, trees, and the ground. It is best recognized by its many oval, entire, opposite, 1"–3" leaves and is easy to find because few vines bloom in the deep shade of much of the towpath north of Seneca. The 1"–2" long flower is two-lipped and becomes yellow with age. The tube is sometimes reddish. From Asia. Brought to America for its fragrant blooms, it escaped and reproduced so well that it has become a pest, especially in wooded areas of the Southeastern United States. (May–Oct., Honeysuckle)

4. **Water Willow** *(Justicia americana)* has flowers with three-lobed lower lips, white (or pale violet) with purple spots, and curved two-lobed upper lips. Flowers grow in close clusters on a 2'–3' tall plant with abundant, opposite, entire, lance-shaped leaves much like those of the willow tree. It may be found between the towpath and the canal, often in the water near Swain's Lock, south of Seneca. (May–July, Acanthus)

5. **Basil Balm** *(Monarda clinopodia)* has a 1'–3' stem topped by a whorl of white or pinkish two-lipped flowers (about 1" long) with small red spots. The oval leaves are opposite, stalked, and toothed. The leaflike bracts under the flowers are often whitish. (June–Aug., Mint)
Wild Bergamot *(Monarda fistulosa)* is similar in structure but its flowers are pinkish or pale lilac and unspotted. (June–Aug., Mint)

6. **Beef-steak** *(Perilla frutescens)* is a 1'–3' plant that usually grows in clumps. Its 3"–5" leaves are numerous, opposite, long-stalked, oval, blunt-toothed, and may have a purple tinge. The ¼" flowers are five-lobed, slightly two-lipped, white (occasionally blue) on the inside and reddish or red-spotted on the outside. They hug 2"–5" spikes that grow from the leaf axils and terminate the stem. From India. (Aug.–Oct., Mint)

7. **Dutchman's Breeches** *(Dicentra cucullaria)*, less than 12" tall, has a cluster of ½" yellow-tipped flowers at the end of a longish stalk. Each flower resembles a pair of pants hung up by their legs to dry; the "legs" are spreading spurs at the top of each. The long-stalked leaves rise from the base of the plant. They are divided several times into narrow, almost fernlike segments. (Mar.–May, Poppy)
Squirrel Corn *(Dicentra canadensis)* differs essentially in that its flowers have spurs that are noticeably shorter and more rounded. The common name comes from the shape of the tubers of this species. It is less frequently found. (Mar.–May, Poppy)

8. **White Clover** *(Trifolium repens)* has stems that creep along the ground, take root, and form large clumps. From these stems rise leaves on long stalks. Growing on even longer stalks are ½"–1" balls of small white (or pale pink) pealike flowers. The leaves are divided into three oval leaflets, each with a pale triangular mark on it. From Europe. The nectar is a good source of honey, and the plant is a desirable forage crop. (May–Sept., Pea)

FLOWERS REGULAR

Parts Easy to Count

9. **Hairy Bitter Cress** (*Cardamine hirsuta*) is 3"–12" tall, and usually grows in clumps, with small white four-petaled flowers at its top, each on a short stem. Flowers are soon surpassed by ½"–1" long, slim, black seed pods. There are a few alternate, upright stem leaves with several narrow leaflets. The basal leaves by contrast, have many pairs of small, roundish leaflets and a larger terminal leaflet. From Europe. The common name comes from the presence of a few hairs at the base of each leaf stalk. (Mar.–Apr., Mustard)

10. **Garlic Mustard** (*Alliaria officinalis*) is 1'–3' tall with a loose cluster of ¼"–⅓" four-petaled flowers at the top. Its alternate leaves are long-stalked, coarsely toothed, and triangular or broadly heart-shaped. The slim, erect 2"–3" seed pods are noticeable. From Europe. The leaves smell like garlic when crushed and have been used as a salad green. It is one of the commonest plants seen along the towpath. (Apr.–July, Mustard)

11. **Multiflora Rose** (*Rosa multiflora*) has clusters of fragrant five-petaled flowers about 1" wide. The tip of each petal is noticeably indented. The plant has slender, arching, or trailing woody stems with alternate leaves usually divided into seven-to-nine oval, toothed leaflets. Brought from Europe for hedges, which sheltered birds and small animals, and as the stock on which commercial roses are grafted, it has escaped to become a pest in many areas. (May, Rose)

12. **Common Blackberry** (*Rubus allegheniensis*) has erect or arched, woody, 2'–8' stems with many flowers. The alternate leaves are divided into three or five (usually five on the main stem and three on its branches), oval, toothed leaflets; the terminal leaflet is the largest. The flower is about 1" wide with five petals. (May–June, Rose)

13. **Aniseroot** *(Osmorhiza longistylis)*, a 1½'–3' plant, has
    several loose clusters of small five-petaled flowers at its
    top. The alternate leaves are divided into three leaflets,
    each deeply lobed and toothed. The lower leaves may
    be 1' or more long. The root is carrotlike and has the
    odor of anise. (May–June, Parsley)
    Honewort *(Cryptotaenia canadensis)* is very similar to
    Aniseroot except for its leaflets which are shallowly
    toothed and only occasionally lobed. (May–July,
    Parsley)

14. **Wild Potato Vine** *(Ipomoea pandurata)* trails on the
    ground or climbs up trees and shrubs. The flowers are
    white with purple or pink striped, or reddish throats.
    Their petals are joined in a funnel shape, 2"–3" wide
    and long, on stalks from the leaf axils. The leaves are
    heart-shaped, entire, and long-stalked. The common
    name comes from the root which grows straight down
    for 1'–2' and is edible. (June–Sept., Morning Glory)
    Hedge Bindweed *(Convolvulus sepium)* is a vine with
    flowers similar to those of No. 14. Those on the
    towpath are usually white but they may be pinkish. Its
    2"–5" long leaves are stalked, arrow-shaped, and entire.
    From Europe. (May–Sept., Morning Glory)

15. **Ox-eye Daisy** *(Chrysanthemum leucanthemum)*, a 1'–3'
    plant, has flowers about 2" wide with fifteen-to-thirty
    rays around a small yellow disk. The deep green
    alternate leaves are 2"–6" long, narrow, toothed, or
    even-lobed. From Europe. (May–Sept., Daisy)

16. **Horse Nettle** *(Solanum carolinense)*, a 1'–3' plant, has
    star-shaped, five-petaled, white (sometimes pale violet)
    1" flowers growing in small clusters. It has alternate,
    irregularly lobed or toothed, oval, 3"–5" leaves. Its
    thorny stems distinguish it from other nightshades in
    our area. Its berries are yellow. The plant contains
    solanine, a highly toxic chemical. (June–Sept.,
    Nightshade)

17. **White Avens** *(Geum canadense)* is a branching, 1'–3' tall
    plant. It has five-petaled, ½" flowers growing alone at
    the end of long stalks. They produce seeds with

hooked thorns that catch on fur and clothing. The
alternate, stalked stem leaves usually have three
toothed leaflets. Basal leaves are also stalked and have
a large terminal leaflet and several pairs of smaller
ones. (June–Aug., Rose)

18. **Flowering Spurge** *(Euphorbia corollata)* has minute
    flowers surrounded by five white round bracts that
    look like a ¼″ flower. They grow in loose clusters at the
    top of the branched stems of the 1′–3′ plant. The leaves
    are entire, oval, stalkless, with rounded ends, and
    alternate except for a whorl of small leaves just before
    the branching of the flowering stalks. A broken stem
    reveals a milky sap, which has been used as a laxative,
    hence the common name whose Latin source is also
    that of purge. (June–Oct., Spurge)

19. **Yarrow** *(Achillea millefolium)*, a 1′–3′ plant, has an
    almost flat, dense, terminal cluster (2″–3″ wide) of tiny
    flowers. They have four to six (usually five) rays. Its
    alternate leaves are so finely subdivided as to appear
    fernlike. Imported from Europe by early colonists for
    its many reputed medicinal uses, it recently has been
    proven to be a source for a blood-clotting chemical.
    (June–Oct., Daisy)

20. **Mild Water-pepper** *(Polygonum hydropiperoides)* has
    slender white (sometimes pinkish or greenish) five-
    petaled flowers scattered in clusters along a several
    inch spike. The 6″–30″ plant is weakly erect with
    stalkless, alternate, lance-shaped leaves. At the leaf
    axils are sheaths around the stem with a fringe of
    bristles on their top edge. It may be found growing in
    water. (July–Sept., Smartweed)

21. **Pokeweed** *(Phytolacca americana)* is a bushlike plant with
    reddish stems which may be 10′ tall. The ¼″, five-
    petaled flowers grow on a 3″ nodding spike. They are
    greenish-white or sometimes pinkish. Its alternate,
    stalked leaves are lanceolate or oval, and wavy-edged.
    It produces clusters of purple-black berries. The juice of
    the berries has been used as a dye, an ink, and a food,
    but it is poisonous unless quite carefully prepared.
    (July–Sept., Pokeberry)

22. **Japanese Knotweed** (*Polygonum cuspidatum*) is a large
    4'–10' plant with many, broad, sharp-pointed, alternate
    leaves with rounded teeth. The small, five-petaled,
    greenish-white flowers grow on branched spikes which
    rise mostly from the leaf axils. From Japan. Brought to
    America for gardens and escaped. (Aug.–Sept.,
    Buckwheat)

23. **False Solomon's Seal** (*Smilacina racemosa*) has an
    arching, zigzag, 1'–3' stem. The leaves are 3"–6" long
    and half as wide, alternate, stalkless, and entire. The
    tiny six-petaled flowers grow in a branched, pyramidal
    cluster at the end of the stem and are soon replaced by
    dull red berries. (May, Lily)
    Star-flowered Solomon's Seal (*Smilacina stellata*) is
    identical in appearance except that its flower cluster is
    not branched and its leaves tend to be folded over
    lengthwise. (May, Lily)

24. **White Wood Aster** (*Aster divaricatus*) is 1'–3' tall with
    alternate, stalked, toothed, heart-shaped, large leaves.
    The flowers have few rays for an aster (five to ten) and
    are on erect stalks at the top of the plant, usually
    forming a flat-topped cluster. (Aug.–Oct., Daisy)

25. **Calico Aster, Starved Aster** (*Aster lateriflorus*) is 1'–5'
    tall with branches along which are many small, short-
    stalked flowers, ½"–1" wide, with nine-to-fourteen rays.
    They may be slightly purplish or white, and often have
    a brown-purple disk. The upper leaves are alternate,
    narrow, stalkless, and may have a few teeth. There are
    several other hard to distinguish species of white or
    purplish asters blooming on the towpath in the fall,
    though not many. (Aug.–Oct., Daisy)

26. **Enchanter's Nightshade** (*Circaea quadrisulcata*) is 1'–3'
    tall with long-stalked (except topmost ones), shallowly
    and irregularly toothed, egg-shaped, opposite leaves.
    The flowers are very small with two deeply notched
    petals, are scattered on up to 6" spikes from the upper
    leaf axils, and terminate the stems. (June–Sept.,
    Evening Primrose)

27. **Virgin's Bower** (*Clematis virginiana*) is a 6'–9' vine that climbs mostly over bushes. The opposite leaves are divided into three coarsely toothed, egg-shaped leaflets. The ½"–1" flowers bloom in a showy cluster and are composed of four widely separated sepals. The seeds have feathery tails. Because of the appearance of the seeds, it is also called "Old Man's Beard." (July–Sept., Buttercup)

28. **Spring Beauty** (*Claytonia virginica*) is 6"–12" tall and often grows in clumps. It has white or pinkish five-petaled flowers, with pink veins. There are two essentially stalkless, narrow, opposite, 3"–7" leaves halfway up the stem. The genus name comes from that of one of the most active plant collectors in the colonies in the eighteenth century, John Clayton of Virginia. (Mar.–May, Purslane)

29. **Field Chickweed** (*Cerastium arvense*) is under 1' tall, and often forms a mat. It has opposite, narrow, entire, stalkless 1"–2" leaves. The approximately 1" wide flowers grow at the top of the stem and have five petals, each split down the center a little less than halfway. From Europe. (Apr.–June, Pink)

30. **Star Chickweed** (*Stellaria pubera*), a sprawling or erect plant which may be up to 16" tall, has a ½" flower with five petals so deeply divided that they often look like ten. The 1"–3" long opposite leaves are mostly without stalks, oblong or oval and entire. (Apr.–June, Pink)
    Common Chickweed (*Stellaria media*) is a smaller, sprawling plant with few or no petals on its tiny ¼" flowers. It is commonly found on lawns and in gardens. (Mar.–Oct., Pink)

31. **Bouncing Bet, Soapwort** (*Saponaria officinalis*) is 1'–3' tall, topped by a loose, round cluster of 1" flowers with five petals that are well separated, slightly reflexed, and indented at the tips. They may be pink or white. The 2"–3" long opposite leaves are oval to lanceolate, stalkless, and have three prominent veins. From Europe. A garden escape whose leaves, when crushed in water, produce a soapy lather. (June–Sept., Pink)

32. **White Vervain** *(Verbena urticifolia)* is a fragile-looking plant, 2'–5' tall, terminating in long, slender spikes of tiny, five-lobed, widely scattered flowers. Flowers also rise from the upper leaf axils. The 3"–7" long, opposite leaves are egg-shaped and coarsely toothed. (June–Oct., Vervain)

33. **Galinsoga** *(Galinsoga ciliata)*, a 6"–18" plant, has ¼" flowers with five (sometimes four) three-toothed rays surrounding a yellow disk. The 1"–2" leaves are opposite, egg-shaped, toothed, and have short stalks. The stem is hairy. (June–Nov., Daisy)
    Galinsoga *(Galinsoga parviflora)* is very similar except its rays are shorter and it has few if any hairs on its stems. Both are from Latin America but common in America and in Europe. (June–Nov., Daisy)

34. **Cut-leaved Toothwort** *(Dentaria laciniata)* is a 9"–15" plant with four-petaled, tubular, ½" long flowers growing in small, terminal clusters. The three stem leaves are whorled. Each is divided into three narrow, toothed leaflets. (Mar.–May, Mustard)
    Slender Toothwort *(Dentaria heterophylla)* may occasionally be found. It is much the same as the Cut-leaved Toothwort, but has only a pair of divided stem leaves. (Apr.–May, Mustard)

35. **Cleavers** *(Galium aparine)* is best distinguished from several other, less common types of bedstraws or cleavers on the towpath by its whorls of usually eight, 1"–3" long, narrow leaves whose edges and stalks bear hooked spines that help it climb over and hang onto other plants. The ⅛" flowers have four petals and grow on stalks from the leaf axils which are longer than the leaves. The plants were used by early American settlers to stuff mattresses; they used the sap to coagulate milk and blood. (May–June, Madder)

36. **Small Water Plantain** *(Alisma subcordatum)* has 6"–1' long, entire, basal, egg-shaped leaves. The small flowers have three round petals, and grow at the ends of the stems of the many-branched 1'–3' plant. It grows in mud or shallow water, usually in the canal bed. The

bulbous base of the plant has been used as a medicine
and as a starchy vegetable. (June–Sept., Arrowhead)

37. **Common Arrowhead** (*Sagittaria latifolia*) grows up to 4'
tall in shallow water or swamplike areas like the canal
bed. The 1"–1½" three-petaled flowers usually grow in
whorls of three. The basal leaves are arrow-shaped, of
varying width, and up to 1' long. American Indians
and early settlers used the tuberous roots as an
important source of food starch. (July–Sept., Water
Plantain)

38. **Wild Strawberry** (*Fragaria virginiana*) has ½"–1" white,
five-petaled flowers, usually in a cluster, growing on a
2"–6" stem that rises from the roots. The leaves are also
basal, each with three coarsely toothed, egg-shaped
leaflets. The plant spreads mostly by runners. The
seeds of this familiar red fruit are scattered on its
surface. Herbal remedies for a wide variety of ailments
such as cataracts, kidney stones, gout, and mouth
sores have been made from the leaves or roots. (Apr.–
June, Rose)

39. **Star-of-Bethlehem** (*Ornithogalum umbellatum*) has a six-
petaled flower, 1" wide, which opens only in the sun.
The petals have a green line in the center of their
undersides. The plant may be 4"–12" tall with grasslike
leaves, mostly at the base of the stem. From Europe.
(May, Lily)

40. **Mayapple, Mandrake** (*Podophyllum peltatum*) is first
seen as two 8"–12", flat, roundish, lobed leaves, rising
10"–15" above the ground. Under the leaves is a 2"
waxy, white flower with six-to-nine petals. The fruits
are yellow. Plants can be found at various points under
the trees on the river side of the towpath. It has had
many medicinal uses, and the berries make good jams
and jellies. (Apr.–May, Barberry)

Parts Hard to Count

41. **Daisy Fleabane** (*Erigeron annuus*) is a 1'–4' plant with
white to pinkish 1" flowers growing close together at

the top of its unbranched stem. Each has over fifty narrow rays surrounding a central yellow disk. The 1"–2" long upper leaves are alternate, stalkless, lance-shaped, and toothed. The name originated in the belief that when the daisies were dried and burned, their smoke repelled insects. (May–Sept., Daisy)
Lesser Daisy Fleabane *(Erigeron strigosus)* is very similar but has upper leaves with no or very few teeth and is not over 2' tall. (May–Sept., Daisy)

42. **Wild Carrot, Queen Anne's Lace, Bird's Nest** *(Daucus carota)* is a 2'–3' tall plant topped by an almost flat, 2"–5" cluster of tiny flowers. After blooming they curl up to form what looks like a bird's nest. The alternate, oblong leaves are finely divided several times into linear segments. From Europe. Closely related to the domestic carrot; the roots may be eaten. (May–Oct., Parsley)

43. **Arrow-leaved Tearthumb** *(Polygonum sagittatum)* has tiny flowers (they may be whitish or greenish) in small clusters on a spike at the top of its 2'–6' stem. There are infrequent, narrow, alternate, 1"–3" leaves on short stalks. Two extensions at the leaf base reach beyond the stem, giving each leaf the appearance of an arrow. Found in or close by the water of the canal. The common name comes from the sharp prickles along the stem. (June–Oct., Smartweed)
Halberd-leaved Tearthumb *(Polygonum arifolium)* is a similar but larger plant with 2"–6" leaves. Leaf extensions are to the side, giving leaves the halberd appearance. (June–Aug., Smartweed)

44. **Tall Meadow-rue** *(Thalictrum polygamum)* is 3'–8' tall and may have white blooms scattered almost all over it. One does not see, in fact, flower petals but the stamens on male plants and the pistils on female ones. The alternate leaves are light green, divided and then subdivided into roundish three-lobed leaflets. (June–Aug., Buttercup)

45. **Lizard's Tail** *(Saururus cernuus)* is a 2'–4' branched plant with one or two 2"–6" spikes of densely packed

flowers ending with a curved top. The spike is white, but it is the color of the stamens and not of petals or sepals as there are none of either. It may be found just south of Seneca Creek in the canal bed and just north of Lock 5 between the towpath and the river. (June–July, Lizard's Tail)

46. **Sweet Everlasting** (*Gnaphalium obtusifolium*), an erect 1'–2' wooly plant, is gray-green or white and has alternate, lance-shaped, stalkless leaves. It has a branched cluster of many small, oval flowers with no distinguishable petals. The base of each flower is enclosed by scaly, yellowish bracts. (Aug.–Sept., Daisy)

47. **Common Elderberry** (*Sambucus canadensis*) is a 3'–10' bush with large opposite leaves divided into five-to-eleven (usually seven) coarsely-toothed leaflets. There are many small white flowers in dense, rather flat clusters, 3"–6" wide. The berries are small and purple-black. (June–July, Honeysuckle)

48. **White Snakeroot** (*Eupatorium rugosum*) may be 1'–4' tall with a compact terminal cluster of tiny flowers. The opposite leaves are sharply toothed and on 1"–2" stalks. It has been used to cure snake bites but is itself somewhat poisonous. (July–Oct., Daisy)
    Boneset (*Eupatorium perfoliatum*) has almost identical flowers but its leaves are joined together around the stem. (Aug.–Sept., Daisy)
    Upland boneset (*Eupatorium sessifolium*) also has similar flowers but its leaves are stalkless, and rounded at their bases. (Aug.–Sept., Daisy)

49. **Buttonbush** (*Cephalanthus occidentalis*) is a 3'–10' bush, growing in wet places with 3"–6" long, entire, egg-shaped leaves that may be opposite or whorled. The ⅓" long flowers that make up the ball-like heads are about 1" in diameter, and tubular. (June–Aug., Madder)

The following species listed under other colors may also be white or whitish: 80, 82, 85, 102, 105, 110, 118.

YELLOW-ORANGE

FLOWERS IRREGULAR

50. **Yellow Sweet Clover** *(Melilotus officinalis)* is much like the white species (see No. 1) but usually is not as tall and blooms somewhat later. From Europe where it is grown for fodder, to produce an insecticide, and as an ingredient for a cheese flavoring. (June–Aug., Pea)

51. **Pale Touch-Me-Not, Jewelweed** *(Impatiens pallida)*, a spreading and open plant, grows 2'–5' tall. The alternate leaves are egg-shaped, coarsely toothed, and grow on a thick stalk. Its pale yellow, 1" long flowers hang from the branches. Each has a spur at the back that turns down. The fruit is purple. It is most often found on the river side of the towpath. For uses see No. 52. (June–Sept., Touch-me-not)

52. **Spotted Touch-Me-Not, Jewelweed** *(Impatiens capensis)* is similar to Pale Touch-Me-Not except that its flower is orange with reddish spots in its throat and its spur is turned around to run parallel to the flower. It is found most often on the canal side of the towpath, at least below Seneca. (June–Sept., Touch-me-not)
The juice from the stems of both species (Nos. 51, 52) is used to limit itching produced by poison ivy. The names Touch-me-not and Impatiens are well deserved. The seed pods explode when touched even lightly, thus spreading wide their seeds.

53. **Sensitive Plant** *(Cassia nictitans)* grows about 1'–2' high with inconspicuous ¼" wide five-petaled flowers in the leaf axils. One petal is twice as long as the others. The 2"–5" long leaves are conspicuous, with eight to fifteen pairs of narrow leaflets. True to the name, the plant's leaflets usually fold up when touched. (Aug.–Oct., Pea)
Partridge Pea *(Cassia fasciculata)* is a very similar plant but is larger and has 1"–1½" flowers, whose petals are about equal in size. (Aug.–Oct., Pea)

FLOWERS REGULAR

Parts Easy to Count

54. Celandine *(Chelidonium majus)* has pale yellow, ¾"
wide, four-petaled flowers clustered near its top. They
produce a 1"–2", upright seed pod. The alternate leaves
are irregularly lobed. From Europe. The stem juice has
been used as a yellow dye, to remove warts and
freckles, and to treat sore eyes. It is poisonous. (May–
Aug., Poppy)

55. Common Evening Primrose *(Oenothera biennis)* is 1'–6'
tall with 1"–2" flowers with four petals, which rise on
short stalks from the axils of the upper leaves. The
stigma is shaped like a cross. The sepals are reflexed,
and the ends of the petals usually indented. The leaves
are alternate, lance-shaped, wavy-edged, and entire or
slightly toothed. The flowers open fully only at
twilight, hence the common name. (July–Sept.,
Evening Primrose)

56. Small-flowered Buttercup *(Ranunculus abortivus)* is
branched and 6"–24" tall. Most of its basal leaves are
roundish, toothed, and indented where attached to
their stalks, but the stem leaves are stalkless, alternate,
and divided into several narrow segments. The five-
petaled flowers are only ¼"–⅜" wide. (April–May,
Buttercup)
Bulbous Buttercup *(Ranunculus bulbosus)* has a shiny,
larger, 1" wide flower. All of its basal leaves are
divided into three deeply toothed segments. It can be
distinguished from other, similar buttercups by its
reflexed sepals. From Europe. (April–May, Buttercup)

57. Common Cinquefoil *(Potentilla simplex)* is an almost
prostrate plant. Each leaf is on a several inch stalk and
has five leaflets, palmately arranged, and toothed for
more than one-half of their length. The five-petaled
flowers are ¼"–½" wide growing on long stalks from
the leaf axils. (Apr.–June, Rose)

Rough Cinquefoil *(Potentilla norvegica)* in contrast is an erect, branched plant, as much as 2' tall. Its leaves are divided into three toothed leaflets. (May–Sept., Rose)

58. **Indian Strawberry** *(Duchesnea indica)* looks much like a strawberry plant, hugs the ground, and has alternate leaves divided into three oval, toothed, leaflets. However, its ½", five-petaled flower is yellow instead of white. The leaflike, three-toothed bracts under each petal are distinctive. From Asia. The red fruit resembles a small strawberry but is tasteless. (May–Aug., Rose)

59. **Yellow Wood-sorrel** *(Oxalis europaea)* has three-lobed, cloverlike, drooping leaves on longish stalks, and a loose cluster of five-petaled flowers, ⅓"–½" wide on similar stalks. The short, slim seed pods grow upright on stalks that are horizontal or bend upward. The 6"–15" tall plant is delicate in appearance. (May–Sept., Wood-sorrel)

60. **Common Mullein** *(Verbascum thapsus)* is a coarse, wooly, 2'–8' plant with a clublike, closely packed spike of buds, seed pods, and a few 1", five-petaled flowers with red spots in their centers. The leaves are largest at the base of the plant, often up to 1' long. They are all white, wooly, oblong, alternate, entire, and stalkless. From Europe. Ancient Greeks used the thick leaves as wicks for their lamps, and the Romans dipped the flower spikes in suet to make torches for funeral processions. The flowers have been used to make a yellow dye. (June–Sept., Figwort)

61. **Virginia Ground-cherry** *(Physalis virginiana)* has greenish yellow, five-petaled, bell-shaped, 1" flowers with purplish spots in their centers hanging singly from the leaf axils. The seed when ripe is enclosed in a greenish, angled bladder about 1" in diameter. The many oval or lance-shaped, long-stalked, alternate leaves may have scattered, shallow teeth or none. (July–Aug., Nightshade)

62. **Golden Ragwort** *(Senecio aureus)* is 1'–2' tall with conspicuous clusters of flowers with six-to-thirteen ½"

or smaller rays. It is distinguished by its long-stalked, round or egg-shaped, blunt-toothed, basal leaves, which contrast with its alternate, lance-shaped, sharply lobed, usually stalkless, stem leaves. (Apr.–May, Daisy)

63. **Wingstem** *(Actinomeris alternifolia)* is the easiest to identify and the most common of five similar species of the daisy family. Its flowers resemble small sunflowers and grow on tall plants that line the towpath in the fall. (See also No. 67). Its 8″, opposite, lance-shaped leaves continue down the stem to make the ¼″–⅓″ wings from which the species gets its common name. The flowers have up to ten, 1″–2″ rays which droop a bit making the pale yellow disk stand out. (Aug.–Oct., Daisy)
Green-headed Coneflower *(Rudbeckia laciniata)* has six to ten of the same sort of rays and a prominent, greenish disk. The stem has no wings and its leaves are usually deeply divided into at least three lobes, each toothed or further lobed. (July–Sept., Daisy)

64. **Fringed Loosestrife** *(Lysimachia ciliata)* is a 1′–3′ plant with ½″–1″, five-petaled flowers on rather long stems growing from the upper leaf axils. They are notable for facing more down than sideward. The petals end in a sharp point. The opposite leaves are oval with pointed tips. (June–Aug., Primrose)

65. **Common St. Johnswort** *(Hypericum perforatum)* has flowers similar to No. 64, but they face sideward and have a noticeable cluster of stamens at their centers. The petals have tiny black dots on their edges. The opposite leaves are oval, not over 1½″ long, entire, and stalkless. From Europe. (June–Sept., St. Johnswort)
Spotted St. Johnswort *(Hypericum punctatum)* has black dots all over the backs of the flowers and black-dotted 2″–3″ long leaves. (June–Sept., St. Johnswort)

66. **Nodding Bur Marigold** *(Bidens cernua)* is 6″–36″ high with opposite, stalkless, narrow, toothed leaves. The six-to-eight rays are short or sometimes missing, producing flowers ½″–1½″ wide. After flowering they nod, hence the common name. (Aug.–Oct., Daisy)

67. **Thin-leaved Sunflower** *(Helianthus decapetalus)* is the commonest of three species found on the towpath. It has 1½"–4" flowers with eight-to-fifteen rays that normally stand out (in contrast to No. 63). Its leaves are opposite and toothed. The lower leaves have stalks of over ¼", usually much longer, and are thin and smooth (July–Oct., Daisy)
    Woodland Sunflower *(Helianthus divaricatus)* has lower leaves with almost no stalks that are rough to the touch. (July–Oct., Daisy)
    Jerusalem Artichoke *(Helianthus tuberosus)*, 6'–10' tall, has lance-shaped leaves, that are well-stalked, very coarsely toothed, thick, and rough. They usually are alternate, but some may be opposite. The stem is hairy. The flowers may have ten-to-twenty rays. It is established as a wildflower in Europe, having been taken to England in the sixteenth century for its edible roots. (Aug.–Oct., Daisy)

68. **Large-flowered Leafcup** *(Polymnia uvedalia)* is a large, coarse plant, 3'–10' tall, with 6"–12" lobed leaves on winged stalks. The scattered, 1½"–3" flowers have ten-to-fifteen widely separated rays. The fruit is used to make jelly and preserves. (July–Sept., Daisy)

69. **Day Lily** *(Hemerocallis fulva)* has an orange, funnel-shaped, six-petaled, 3"–4" flower on a stem 2'–3' long; the flower lasts one day. The narrow basal leaves are about 2'–3' long. Brought from Asia for gardens and escaped, but usually found only near former dwellings along the canal. (June–Aug., Lily)

70. **Spatterdock** *(Nuphar variegatum)* has 6"–12" wide, heart-shaped leaves that usually float on stagnant, shallow water. The 2"–3" wide, yellow flower rises above them here and there. Curved, upright, sepals are visible making a rounded cup that almost hides the large disk in the flower's center. It can be found in the ponds on the river side of the towpath at Widewater. (May–Sept., Water Lily)

71. **Dog-tooth Violet, Yellow Adder's Tongue, Trout Lily** *(Erythronium americanum)* has two 3"–8" oval, entire,

basal leaves, usually mottled green and brown. A
single flower droops at the end of a 3"–6" stem. Its six
yellow, separated petals turn back. They often are
spotted at their bases or are darker on their reverse
sides. The plants usually grow in clumps. The several
popular names reflect, respectively, the shape of the
root structure and the color of a European species; the
appearance of the leaves when they first come through
the ground; and the resemblance of the leaf mottling to
that on some trouts. (Apr.–May, Lily)

Parts Hard to Count

72. **Rough-stemmed Goldenrod** (*Solidago rugosa*), a 1'–7'
    plant, has flowers with six-to-ten rays along the upper
    side of arched stems at its top. Its alternate, lance-
    shaped, stalkless leaves are all about the same size,
    deeply toothed, and wrinkled. The stem is very hairy.
    (Aug.–Oct., Daisy)
    Early Goldenrod (*Solidago juncea*) is similar except that
    its upper leaves grow gradually smaller and are hardly
    toothed if at all. The stem is hairless. (July–September,
    Daisy)

73. **Blue-stemmed Goldenrod** (*Solidago caesia*) has arched
    stems similar to No. 72, but the three-to-four rayed
    flowers are confined to clusters at each leaf axil. The
    alternate leaves are sharply toothed and gradually
    reduce in size toward the top of the plant. The stem is
    slightly bluish. There are a number of other plants of
    this genus to be found along the towpath but none in
    great numbers. All are characterized by small flowers
    with three-to-twelve rays and usually lance-shaped
    leaves, making exact identification difficult. (Sept.–Oct.,
    Daisy)

74. **Spanish Needles** (*Bidens bipinnata*) has no ray flowers
    so one can see only a spot or so of yellow on the small
    disk. Its seeds have three-to-four short barbs on their
    tops that catch on fur or clothing. Its 4"–8" long leaves

are deeply divided into many narrow segments and closely resemble fern leaves. (Aug.–Oct., Daisy)

Beggar-ticks *(Bidens frondosa)* has similar flowers but its leaves are divided into three-to-five toothed leaflets. (Sept.–Oct., Daisy)

Tall Beggar-ticks *(Bidens vulgata)* is similar to the preceding species except that it has ten-to-twenty, instead of five-to-nine, leaflike bracts under each flower. (Sept.–Oct., Daisy)

75. **King Devil, Field Hawkweed** *(Hieracium pratense)* has a 1'–3' stem on the top of which are four or more ¾" flowers with overlapping rays. The basal, entire, lanceolate leaves are several inches long. The entire plant is covered with stiff, black, gland-tipped hairs. From Europe. (May–Aug., Daisy)

The following species listed under other colors may also be yellow or orange: 3.

PINK-RED

FLOWERS IRREGULAR

76. **Red Clover** *(Trifolium pratense)* has tiny flowers clustered in a ball about 1" in diameter at the top of the stem. They are pealike and reddish-purple. The leaves are divided into three leaflets, each of which usually has a pale "V" in its center. The plant is 6"–18" tall. From Europe. Brought for forage and escaped. The leaves were used by American Indians in salads and soups. (May–Oct., Pea)

77. **Hoary Tick Trefoil** *(Desmodium canascens)* is 3'–5' tall and has hairy stems. Its leaflets are egg-shaped and of equal size. It is the most common of several Desmodium species found along the towpath. The species share common characteristics and are not easy to distinguish from each other. They all have loose clusters of pealike, ⅓", pink flowers. All are branching plants with alternate leaves divided into three entire leaflets growing on very short stalks. All have conspicuous seed pods with three or more separated sections. (July–Oct., Pea)
Showy Tick Trefoil *(Desmodium canadense)* has flowers that grow close together, lancelike leaves, and downy rather than hairy stems. (July–Oct., Pea)
Panicled Tick Trefoil *(Desmodium paniculatum)* has a terminal leaflet four times as long as wide and a many-branched flower spike. (July–Oct., Pea)

78. **Cardinal Flower** *(Lobelia cardinalis)*, a 2'–4' plant, has two-lipped flowers, the reddest on the towpath, which grow on short stalks on a terminal spike. The plant has alternate, lance-shaped, toothed leaves. The bright red attracts hummingbirds to act as pollinators. Not common, but found between the towpath and the river north of Lock 5 and in the bed of the lock at Spring Gap. (July–Sept., Bellflower)

FLOWERS REGULAR

Parts Easy to Count

79. **Swamp Rose** (*Rosa palustris*) is a bushy, 2'–8' shrub whose upper branches have scattered, stout, usually hooked prickles. The pink flower is 2"–3" wide, with five petals slightly indented at their tips, and a large cluster of yellow stamens in its center. The alternate leaves are divided into three-to-nine, (usually seven) finely toothed leaflets. Not common, but found along Widewater and at Edwards Ferry. (May–June, Rose)

80. **Halberd-leaved Rose Mallow** (*Hibiscus militaris*) is a 3'–7' plant whose 3"–6" alternate leaves are shaped somewhat like a halberd with pointed wings on each side of their bases. The 4"–6" wide, five-petaled flowers usually have a purplish center. They may be white or pink. As in all mallows, the stamens are joined together to form a 2"–3" column in the center of the flower. (July–Sept., Mallow)
    Swamp Rose Mallow (*Hibiscus palustris*) differs essentially in having rounded leaves, almost as broad as long, without pointed wings at their bases. (July–Sept., Mallow)
    Both may grow on the edge of the canal and were used as herbal medicines for a wide variety of complaints from bee stings to baldness.

81. **Trumpet Creeper** (*Campsis radicans*) is a vine that climbs over rocks and up tree trunks to display its 3", trumpet-shaped, five-petaled flowers. It may be 30' or more long. The opposite leaves are divided into seven-to-eleven leaflets. (June–Aug., Bignonia)

82. **Dame's Rocket** (*Hesperis matronalis*) has four-petaled, ¾"–1" flowers growing in clusters at the top of its 1'–3' stem and on stalks from the upper leaf axils. They may be pink, purplish, or white. The opposite leaves are

stalked, lance-shaped, and finely toothed. In general
appearance it resembles Garden Phlox but blooms
much earlier. From Europe. Brought to America for
gardens, and escaped. (May–June, Mustard)

83. **Deptford Pink** *(Dianthus armeria)*, a 1'–2' plant, is
topped by deep pink flowers with white spots in a
loose cluster. The five petals end in small teeth. There
are a few opposite, narrow, entire leaves on the stem
and at the base of the plant. From Europe. Brought to
America for gardens and escaped. Many grew wild
around the London suburb of Deptford. (June–Sept.,
Pink)

84. **Swamp Milkweed** *(Asclepias incarnata)* a branched, 2'–4'
tall plant has a close, terminal cluster of rose-purple to
pink flowers. Each is peculiarly shaped with five petals
pointed downward, and five upright, hoodlike
structures. The leaves are opposite, entire, and nearly
lance-shaped. A broken stem reveals a milky sap. The
seeds are encased in a large, oblong pod. Found in the
Lock 5 area and very sparingly up to Great Falls.
(June–Aug., Milkweed)
Common Milkweed *(Asclepias syriaca)* is a similiar plant
but its flowers are brownish-purple, and often grow in
a drooping cluster. Its leaves are wider, and its 2"–3"
pods have a warty surface. The milky nature of the sap
was taken as a sign by American Indians that it would
increase the flow of milk from lactating mothers. It was
also used to treat dropsy, for which we now know it
possesses the proper chemicals. (June–Aug., Milkweed)

85. **Garden Phlox** *(Phlox paniculata)* is an erect, 2'–6' tall,
unbranched plant with opposite, stalkless leaves three-
to-four times as long as wide. The magenta-pink,
(sometimes shading toward white) five-petaled flowers
grow in a large cluster at the top of the plant. It had
many medical uses in earlier times. (July–Sept., Phlox)

Parts Hard to Count

86. **Nodding Thistle** (*Carduus nutans*) has a tight 2″ wide cluster of reddish-purple flowers that droops or nods. Just under it are rows of spiny, reflexed, purplish bracts. The alternate leaves are up to 10″ long, deeply lobed, and have spiny teeth with rows of the spines running down the main stem. The plant may be 4′ or more tall. From Europe. (June–Oct., Daisy)

87. **Lady's Thumb** (*Polygonum persicaria*) is an erect or sprawling 6″–24″ plant that tends to grow in clumps. Its tiny pink or rose flowers grow in a tight, stout spike. The alternate leaves are narrow and stalkless. Each has a dark triangular blotch in its center that is sometimes hard to see. A short sheath, topped by a fringe, encircles the usually reddish stem where each leaf joins it. From Europe. (July–Oct., Buckwheat)

88. **Spotted Joe-pye-weed** (*Eupatorium maculatum*) is a 3′–7′ tall plant with leaves in whorls of four or five. Its stem is purple or purple-spotted. The small, dull pink-purple flowers are in a close, flattish cluster. (July–Sept., Daisy)
    Hollow Joe-pye-weed (*Eupatorium fistulosum*) is similar except that it has four-to-seven (usually six) whorled leaves, a stem tinged (not spotted) with purple, and flowers in a dome-shaped cluster. (July–Sept., Daisy)
    Purple Joe-pye-weed (*Eupatorium purpureum*) has a stem that is purple only where the leaves join it. The whorls are composed mostly of three or four leaves. The flowers grow in a dome like that of the Hollow Joe-pye-weed. (July–Sept., Daisy) There is now some doubt as to whether these differences justify separation into three species.

The following species listed under other colors may also be red or pink: 8, 19, 20, 21, 28, 31, 100.

Blue-Purple

FLOWERS IRREGULAR

89. **Cow Vetch, Tufted Vetch** *(Vicia cracca)* has violet-blue
½", pealike flowers growing close together on one side
of its spike, which rises from a leaf axil. The alternate
leaves have eight-to-twelve pairs of narrow, ½" leaflets
and terminate with two tendrils which help the vine
climb onto plants and bushes. From Europe. Brought
for use as a forage crop. The roots, stems, and seeds
were eaten by American Indians. (May–Aug., Pea)

90. **Great Lobelia** *(Lobelia siphilitica)* has one of the largest
of the irregular, two-lipped, 1"–2" long flowers that
characterize this genus. It features blue and white lines
on the underside of the lower lip. The plant may be 1'–
3' tall and has alternate, lance-shaped, and either entire
or irregularly toothed leaves. It was sent to Europe by
early American settlers as a cure for syphilis. However,
it not only failed to work, but produced severe side
effects. Nevertheless, it received its Latin name from
this effort. It can be found near Lock 7, in the Great
Falls area, and at Edwards Ferry. (June–Sept.,
Bellflower)
    Spiked Lobelia *(Lobelia spicata)* has pale blue flowers
less than half as long as those of the Great Lobelia, on
a slender, leafless spike. (June–Aug., Bellflower)

91. **Indian Tobacco** *(Lobelia inflata)* has alternate, oval,
toothed leaves without stalks. The ¼" long flower is
blue, two-lipped (the upper lip has two teeth and the
lower has three), and grows on a very short stalk along
a 6"–36", upright, usually branched stem. There are
conspicuous, round seed pods. American Indians
smoked and chewed its bitter leaves. However, the
leaves can produce such unpleasant reactions that they
have been used as an anti-smoking drug. (July-Sept.,
Bellflower)

92. **Asiatic Dayflower** (*Commelina communis*) has broad,
    lance-shaped leaves that clasp its reclining stem. At its
    tip are ½"–1", three-petaled flowers, the upper two,
    blue and the much smaller, lower one, white. From
    Asia. It is called Dayflower because each flower is open
    only one day. (Aug.–Sept., Spiderwort)

93. **Gill-over-the-Ground, Ground Ivy** (*Glechoma hederacea*)
    is a creeping plant, often covering large areas with its
    alternate, roundish, scalloped, stalked leaves that are
    sometimes tinged with purple. The ⅓"–½" long flowers
    are blue-purple or violet, two-lipped and grow on short
    stalks from the leaf axils. From Europe. It has become
    so common that it has acquired the American
    nickname, "Creeping Charlie." (Apr.–June, Mint)

94. **Purple Dead-Nettle** (*Lamium purpureum*), a 6"–12" tall
    plant, has opposite, roundish, blunt-toothed, stalked
    leaves. The upper leaves are crowded together and are
    usually purplish. The ⅓"–½" flower is purple, two-
    lipped and grows mostly from leaf axils at the top of
    the plant. From Europe. (Apr.–May, Mint)

95. **Self-heal, Heal-all** (*Prunella vulgaris*) has opposite, oval,
    stalked, usually entire leaves on sprawling or erect
    stems. Atop the stems are violet, two-lipped (upper lip
    hood-shaped and lower fringed) flowers in a dense, 1"–
    2" spike. Only a few flowers are out at a time. From
    Europe. It was used in the past to treat a wide variety
    of health problems. (May–Oct., Mint)

96. **Common Speedwell** (*Veronica officinalis*) trails along the
    ground with its ¼" pale violet flowers on 1"–2" spikes
    rising from the leaf axils. The opposite, elliptical,
    toothed leaves are ¾"–2" long on short stalks. It may
    bloom from time to time until late fall. (May–July,
    Figwort)
    Corn Speedwell (*Veronica arvensis*) has single blue
    flowers in the leaf axils that are smaller than those of
    the Common Speedwell. The leaves are also much
    smaller, almost clasping the 1"–6" stem, and have a few
    rounded teeth. From Europe. (Mar.–July, Figwort)

Ivy Speedwell *(Veronica hederaefolia)* is very similar but its flowers have stalks about ⅓"–½" long. From Europe. It grows mostly under the trees between the towpath and the river. (Apr.–May, Figwort)

97. **Hairy Beardtongue** *(Penstemon hirsutus)*, a 1'–3' plant, has slender, two-lipped, ¾"–1" long flowers that are lavender or pale violet, with nearly closed throats. The 1"–2" long leaves are stalkless, toothed, opposite and lance shaped. (June–July, Figwort)
    Gray Beardtongue *(Penstemon canescens)* is very similar but has less slender flowers that have violet stripes inside and open throats. They may be blue-purple as well as pale violet. (June–July, Figwort)

98. **Peppermint** *(Mentha piperita)* has ¼", two-lipped purplish or pale violet flowers in packed whorls on spikes which are both terminal and rise from the leaf axils. The plant is about 1'–3' tall and has a square stem. The opposite leaves are stalked, oval, and toothed. From Europe. The leaves taste like peppermint. (July–Sept., Mint)

99. **Mad-dog Skullcap** *(Scutellaria lateriflora)* has two-lipped, erect, ½" or smaller flowers, usually growing in pairs, on one side of 1"–4" spikes from the leaf axils. The upper lip is hoodlike and the lower one flat and three-lobed. The 2" long leaves are opposite, stalked, egg-shaped, and coarsely toothed. Named for its use by American Indians to treat rabies, hysteria, and convulsions. In part these uses were correct, as an anti-spasmodic drug has been extracted from the dried flowers. (July–Sept., Mint)

100. **Monkey Flower** *(Mimulus ringens)* is 1'–3' tall with square stems and opposite, oval to lanceolate, slightly toothed, stalkless leaves. The 1" flowers are violet or pinkish, two-lipped, on stalks longer than the leaves, and rise from the leaf axils. The lower lip of each flower has three spreading lobes. The throat is partially closed by a yellow, ridged hump. Found in wet places in the Lock 5–7, Widewater and Sharpsburg areas, but there are few examples in each. (July–Aug., Figwort)

101. Common Blue Violet *(Viola papilionacea)* is more purple
than blue. Leaves and flowers are both on long stalks
that grow separately from the roots or base. The leaves
are heart-shaped and toothed. The bottom petal of the
five flower petals extends backward to form a short
spur. The lower two of the side petals have patches of
hair at their bases. The flowers add Vitamin C
palatably to a salad. (Apr.–May, Violet)

FLOWERS REGULAR

Parts Easy to Count

102. Virginia Bluebell *(Mertensia virginica)* has pink buds
and blue (occasionally white) ½"–1" flowers in drooping
clusters. Each flower has five petals joined to form a
trumpetlike bloom. The alternate leaves are oval,
stalked, and entire. It is common in Northern Virginia,
but I have seen it only rarely under the trees on the
river side of the towpath, particularly in the Lock 5–7
and Edwards Ferry areas. It is sometimes called Oyster
Leaf because its leaves taste like oysters. (Apr.–May,
Forget-me-not)

103. Venus's Looking-Glass *(Specularia perfoliata)* has blue or
violet, ½"–¾" flowers with five petals usually growing
singly and stalkless in the axils of the upper leaves.
The ½"–1" long leaves are alternate, heart-shaped,
toothed, and clasp the stem. The plant is unbranched
and may vary from 6"–30" tall. The popular name
comes from the shiny appearance of the flat seed.
(May–Aug., Bluebell)

104. Tall Bellflower *(Campanula americana)* is one of the few
in its family whose flower is not bell-shaped. Five pale
blue petals spread out flat, form flowers about 1" wide
growing on short stalks from the leaf axils on a 2'–6'
unbranched stem. The leaves are alternate, slightly
toothed, and with no or almost no stalks. They become

smaller on the upper parts of the stem. Found on the river side of the towpath between Spring Gap and North Branch. (July–Sept., Bluebell)

105. **Chicory** *(Cichorium intybus)*, a 1'–4' erect plant, has alternate, stalkless, upper leaves which may be toothed, lobed, or entire. The 1"–1½" wide blue flowers are stalkless in the upper leaf axils. The tip of each of the ten-to-fifteen rays is toothed. Each bloom lasts one day. White flowers occur rarely. From Europe. Brought to America because its roots can be used to make a "coffee" drink; they are still so used sometimes. It has become so common along roads and in fields that it is often labeled a weed. (June–Sept., Daisy)

106. **Blue Lettuce** *(Lactuca floridana)* has 3"–6" long, alternate leaves, usually with stalks, and deep, pointed lobes much like those of a dandelion. The white, hairy seeds also resemble those of a dandelion. The flower heads grow in loose clusters at the top of an erect plant which may be as much as 7' tall. In color and structure they resemble those of No. 105 but are smaller, about ½" across, and have eleven-to-seventeen rays. There is no central disk. (Aug.–Oct., Daisy)
Tall Blue Lettuce *(Lactuca biennis)* has similar leaves but is topped by small, ¼" flower heads that grow in a rather tight cluster. The plant may grow to 15'. (Aug.–Oct., Daisy)

107. **Wild Blue Phlox** *(Phlox divaricata)* has opposite, narrow, entire, stalkless leaves that are widest at their bases. The five petals are blue to violet, wedge-shaped, and spread at the end of a tube about as long as the petals. The flowers top an erect, 10"–20" tall plant that usually grows in clumps. (Apr.–May, Phlox)

108. **Larger Blue Flag** *(Iris versicolor)* grows 1'–3' tall with flowers of various shades of violet or purple about 2"–3" wide that have three upright petals and three drooping, reflexed sepals. Each sepal has a yellowish spot at its base. It is the only blue iris in our area. Not common, but can be found at Widewater, Paw Paw, and Spring Gap. (June–Aug., Iris)

Yellow Iris *(Iris pseudacorus)* is similar except for its color. From Europe. I found it only at Edwards Ferry. Both Blue and Yellow Iris grow in wet areas, especially in the canal bed. (May, Iris)

109. **Blue-eyed Grass** *(Sisyrinchium angustifolium)* has one or two long, narrow, grasslike leaves growing from its base. Halfway up the 6″–18″ stem a leaflike bract separates from the stem and one or more flowering, several-inch long stalks rise from the axil. The flower has six blue petal-like parts, each with a bristlelike tip, and a small yellow base. Each bloom lasts only a day. (May, Iris)

Parts Hard to Count

110. **Elephant's-foot** *(Elephantopus carolinianus)* is an erect, 1′–3′ plant, usually branched, with alternate, oval, stalkless leaves which may be 3″–6″ long. The terminal, ½″–1″ blue flower has many narrow rays. Underneath are four triangular leaflike bracts of different sizes. In rare cases the flowers may be white. The name comes from what the collection of bracts under the flower cluster looked like to an early botanist. (July–Sept., Daisy)

111. **New England Aster** *(Aster novae-angliae)* has distinctive 1″–2″ flowers with forty-to-fifty violet-purple rays. It is a stout, 2′–8′ plant with many alternate, entire, lance-shaped leaves that clasp the stem. (Sept.–Nov., Daisy)

112. **Mistflower, Wild Ageratum** *(Eupatorium coelestinum)* is a 1′–3′ plant with toothed, triangular, stalked, opposite leaves. The tiny blue or violet flowers are packed in close, flat clusters at the top of the plant. They look like those of the garden Ageratum. (July–Sept., Daisy)

The following species listed under other colors may also be blue or purple: 6, 25, 82.

FLOWERS IRREGULAR

113. **Wild Ginger** (*Asarum canadense*) has a single pair of
large, heart-shaped, 6"–12" tall leaves from the center of
which a bell-shaped, purple-brown, 1" flower rises on a
short stalk with three rather long, pointed, curved
lobes. The flower is made of sepals, not petals. The
plant is so low that its flower is often covered by old
leaves. The root smells of and tastes like ginger.
American Indians used it as a spice and a medicine.
(Apr.–June, Birthroot)

FLOWERS REGULAR

Parts Easy to Count

114. **Smooth Solomon's Seal** (*Polygonatum biflorum*) has an
unbranched, arching 1'–2' long stem beneath which
hangs a row of ½" or smaller, greenish, bell-like
flowers with six shallow lobes. There are usually one or
two at each leaf axil but there may be as many as four.
The 2"–4" long alternate leaves are egg-shaped, entire,
and almost stalkless. There are blue-black berries.
(Apr.–June, Lily)
Great Solomon's Seal (*Polygonatum canaliculatum*) has a
stout, more erect stem which is over 3' long. The
flowers are usually ½"–1" long and grow in clusters.
(Apr.–June, Lily)
The underground stems of both are edible and the sap
has been used for earache and sunburn.

Parts Hard to Count

115. **Curled Dock** (*Rumex crispus*) is a coarse, 1'–4' plant
with several spikes on which are whorls of short-
stalked small, drooping, green flowers. The leaves are
entire but are curled strongly along the margins. They

are 1' long and several inches wide. From Europe
where the leaves were cooked as a green vegetable.
(May–July, Buckwheat)
Broad-leaved Dock *(Rumex obtusifolius)* has a similar
flower and plant structure, but its basal leaves are
wide, with rounded ends and without curled edges.
From Europe where it was used on nettle stings and
burns. (June–Sept., Buckwheat)

116. **Wood Nettle** *(Laportea canadensis)*, a stout 1'–4' tall
plant, has alternate, stalked, egg-shaped, coarsely
toothed, 3"–6" leaves. The flowers are small and
greenish in loose, branching clusters that grow from
the leaf axils and often rise 4"–6" above the topmost
leaves. The stem is covered with stinging hairs. (July–
Sept., Nettle)

117. **Stinging Nettle** *(Urtica dioica)* may grow to be 6' or
more tall. It is an unbranched plant with opposite, egg-
shaped or narrow, coarsely toothed leaves on short
stalks. Its small greenish flowers grow on slender,
spreading or drooping, branched spikes from the leaf
axils. From Europe where its young tops were eaten
like spinach, its sap used to curdle milk, and fibers
from its stem used to weave fine textiles. Its sting is
caused by crystals of oxalic acid in the bristly hairs on
its stem and leaves. (June–Sept., Nettle)
False Nettle *(Boehmeria cylindrica)* has similar leaves but
its small green flowers grow on straight unbranched
spikes. It does not have stinging hairs. (June–Oct.,
Nettle)

118. **Clearweed** *(Pilea pumila)* is a 1'–1½' plant with
opposite, egg-shaped coarsely toothed, stalked leaves
with noticeably shiny upper surfaces. Each leaf has
three deep veins running through it. Its tiny, whitish
or greenish flowers are on short, curved stalks growing
horizontally from the leaf axils, and are usually hidden
by the many leaves. (Aug.–Sept., Nettle)

119. **Great Ragweed** *(Ambrosia trifida)* is usually 6'–10' tall
but may grow to 15'. It has large, opposite, stalked
leaves with three (sometimes five) distinct lobes, and

rounded teeth. Its tiny greenish flowers are on terminal spikes. (Aug.–Oct., Daisy).

Common Ragweed (*Ambrosia artemisiifolia*) is best distinguished by its leaves which are divided several times into narrow segments. They may be alternate as well as opposite. It does not grow more than 6'. The genus name refers to the use of the seeds in the Middle Ages to brew a popular drink. Today Ragweed is, of course, best known for its pollen, which is the principal cause of hay fever. (Aug.–Oct., Daisy)

120. **Jack-in-the-Pulpit** (*Arisaema triphyllum*) is 1'–3' tall with a unique structure consisting of a greenish or purple-brown canopy curved over a clublike, yellowish spike. On the lower part of the spike are very tiny flowers that produce a cluster of red berries on the female plants in the fall. There are one or two leaves on stalks, each divided into three leaflets. The root and berries were eaten by American Indians who boiled them first to remove irritating crystals. (Apr.–May, Arum)

The following species listed under other colors may also be green or brown: 20, 21, 22, 43, 61.

BIBLIOGRAPHY

Gleason, H.A. *New Britton and Brown Illustrated Flora of the Northeastern United States and Adjacent Canada*. New York and London: Harford, 1968.

Klimas, John E. and James A. Cunningham *Wildflowers of Eastern America*. New York: Alfred A. Knopf, 1968.

Newcomb, Lawrence. *Newcomb's Wildflower Guide*. Boston and Toronto: Little, Brown and Company, 1977.

Peterson, Roger T., and Margaret McKenny. *A Field Guide to Wildflowers of Northeastern and North-Central North America*. Boston: Houghton Mifflin, 1968.

Appendix

COMMON AND LATIN FAMILY NAMES

Acanthus	Acanthaceae
Arum	Araceae
Barberry	Berberidaceae
Bignonia	Bignoniaceae
Birthwort	Aristolochiaceae
Borage	Boraginaceae
Buckwheat	Polygonaceae
Buttercup	Ranunculaceae
Bluebell	Campanulaceae
Daisy	Compositae (Asteraceae)
Evening Primrose	Onagraceae
Figwort	Scrophulariaceae
Honeysuckle	Caprifoliaceae
Iris	Iridaceae
Lily	Liliaceae
Lizard's Tail	Saururaceae
Madder	Rubiaceae
Mallow	Malvaceae
Milkweed	Asclepiadaceae
Mint	Labiatae (Lamiaceae)
Morning Glory	Convolvulaceae
Mustard	Cruciferae (Brassicaceae)
Nettle	Urticaceae
Nightshade	Solanaceae
Parsley	Umbelliferae (Apiaceae)
Pea	Leguminosae (Fabiaceae)
Phlox	Polemoniaceae
Pink	Carophyllaceae
Pokeweed	Phytolaccaceae
Poppy	Papaveraceae
Purslane	Portulacaceae
Rose	Rosaceae

NOTE: Some contemporary botanists use the family names with regular endings, given above in parentheses, in place of the traditional names.

Spiderwort	Commelinaceae
Spurge	Euphorbiaceae
Touch-me-not	Balsaminaceae
Vervain	Verbenaceae
Violet	Violaceae
Water Lily	Nymphaeaceae
Water Leaf	Hydrophyllaceae
Wood Sorrel	Oxalidaceae

INDEX

COLOR ILLUSTRATIONS

1. White Sweet Clover
2. Pale Violet
3. Japanese Honeysuckle
4. Water Willow

5. Basil Balm
6. Beef-steak
7. Dutchman's Breeches
8. White Clover

9. Hairy Bitter Cress
10. Garlic Mustard
11. Multiflora Rose
12. Common Blackberry

13. Aniseroot
14. Wild Potato Vine
15. Ox-eye Daisy
16. Horse Nettle

17. White Avens
18. Flowering Spurge
19. Yarrow
20. Mild Water-pepper

21. Pokeweed
22. Japanese Knotweed
23. False Solomon's Seal
24. White Wood Aster

25. Calico Aster
26. Enchanter's Nightshade
27. Virgin's Bower
28. Spring Beauty

29. Field Chickweed
30. Star Chickweed
31. Bouncing Bet
32. White Vervain

33. Galinsoga
34. Cut-leaved Toothwort
35. Cleavers
36. Small Water Plantain

37. Common Arrowhead
38. Wild Strawberry
39. Star-of-Bethlehem
40. Mayapple

41. Daisy Fleabane
42. Queen Anne's Lace
43. Arrow-leaved Tearthumb
44. Tall Meadow-rue
45. Lizard's Tail
46. Sweet Everlasting
47. Common Elderberry
48. White Snakeroot

49. Buttonbush
50. Yellow Sweet Clover
51. Pale Touch-Me-Not
52. Spotted Touch-Me-Not

53. Sensitive Plant
54. Celandine
55. Common Evening Primrose
56. Small-flowered Buttercup

57. Common Cinquefoil
58. Indian Strawberry
59. Yellow Wood-sorrel
60. Common Mullein

61. Virginia Ground-cherry
62. Golden Ragwort
63. Wingstem
64. Fringed Loosestrife

65. Common St. Johnswort
66. Nodding Bur Marigold
67. Thin-leaved Sunflower
68. Large-flowered Leafcup

69. Day Lily
70. Spatterdock
71. Dog-tooth Violet
72. Rough-stemmed Goldenrod

73. Blue-stemmed Goldenrod
74. Spanish Needles
75. King Devil
76. Red Clover

77. Hoary Tick Trefoil
78. Cardinal Flower
79. Swamp Rose
80. Halberd-leaved Rose Mallow

81. Trumpet Creeper
82. Dame's Rocket
83. Deptford Pink
84. Swamp Milkweed

85. Garden Phlox
86. Nodding Thistle
87. Lady's Thumb
88. Spotted Joe-pye-weed

89. Cow Vetch
90. Great Lobelia
91. Indian Tobacco
92. Asiatic Dayflower

93. Gill-over-the-Ground
94. Purple Dead-Nettle
95. Self-heal
96. Common Speedwell

97. Hairy Beardtongue
98. Peppermint
99. Mad-dog Skullcap
100. Monkey Flower

101. Common Blue Violet
102. Virginia Bluebell
103. Venus's Looking-Glass
104. Tall Bellflower

105. Chicory
106. Blue Lettuce
107. Wild Blue Phlox
108. Larger Blue Flag

109. Blue-eyed Grass
110. Elephant's-foot
111. New England Aster
112. Wild Ageratum

113. Wild Ginger
114. Smooth Solomon's Seal
115. Curled Dock
116. Wood Nettle ⁻

117. Stinging Nettle
118. Clearweed
119. Great Ragweed
120. Jack-in-the-Pulpit